W I L D C A T S !
O F T H E W O R L D

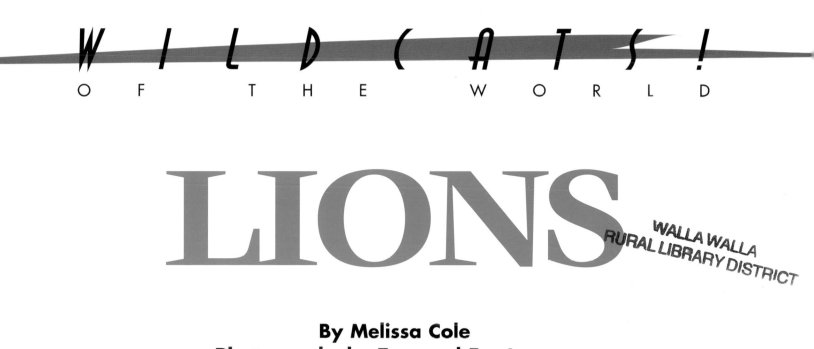

LIONS

By Melissa Cole
Photographs by Tom and Pat Leeson

B L A C K B I R C H P R E S S

GALE GROUP
™
THOMSON LEARNING

Detroit • New York • San Diego • San Francisco
Boston • New Haven, Conn. • Waterville, Maine
London • Munich

Published by Blackbirch Press
10911 Technology Place
San Diego, CA 92127

e-mail: customerservice@galegroup.com
Web site: www.galegroup.com/blackbirch

©2002 by Blackbirch Press
an imprint of the Gale Group
First Edition

Printed in China

10 9 8 7 6 5 4 3 2 1

Library of Congress Cataloging-in-Publication Data
Cole, Melissa
Lions / by Melissa Cole.
        p.   cm. — (Wild cats of the world)
Summary: Describes the physical characteristics, behavior, habitat, and endangered status of lions.
      ISBN 1-56711-448-2 (hardcover : alk. paper)
      1. Lions—Juvenile literature. [1.Lions. 2. Endangered species.]
      I. Title. II. Series.
QL737.C23 C643 2002
599.757—dc21   2001005047

Contents

Introduction

For thousands of years, the lion has been both feared and admired. Ten thousand years ago, lions lived across large areas of the world from Europe to India. Ancient lion fossils have even been found in North America. Today, lions live mainly

Humans both fear and admire lions.

on the grassy savannas and desert areas of Africa. A small population of Asiatic lions lives in the Gir Forest National Park in northwest India.

Lions live mainly on the grasslands of Africa.

The Body of a Lion

Lions are the second largest of the great cats—big cats that roar, but do not purr. Only tigers are bigger. Lions weigh between 300 and 500 pounds (136 and 227 kg). Male lions are often twice as large as female lions, or lionesses. They can be 10 feet (3 m) long from nose to tail.

A female lion is about half the size of a male lion.

Lions have stocky, powerful legs that allow them to reach speeds up to 35 miles (56 km) per hour. Their hooked claws can grasp and slash the animals they hunt. Like most cats, lions can pull their claws into their paws to keep them sharp.

Male lions have a thick mane of dark fur.

Lions have beige-yellow coats that help them hide in the tall grass of the African savanna. By blending in with their surroundings, they are able to get close to their prey.

Lions have long blonde tails with dark tufts of fur on the tip. Their tails help them balance as they chase prey. Scientists also believe that lion cubs follow their mothers through the tall grass by watching the tuft of her tail. Lions also use their tails to express themselves. An angry lion will swish its tail back and forth to show aggression. Curious lions will stick their tails straight up in the air when greeting each other.

Male lions have a shaggy mane of dark hair that covers the neck. This mane makes lions appear larger and more threatening. It also protects the head and neck during fights with other male lions.

Asiatic lions are smaller than African lions. Males have shorter manes and a long fold of skin on their bellies, which most African lions do not have.

Special Features

Lions eat only meat. Their specialized teeth help them eat after they have chased down their prey. Long canine teeth pierce a prey's neck or spinal cord and kill instantly. Cutting teeth shear through skin, fat, and flesh. Molars at the rear of the jaw are strong enough to crack bones.

Lions also have another important tool—the tongue. A lion's tongue is covered with small hook-like bumps called papillae. The hooks are good for scooping up water when lions drink. Papillae also act like the teeth of a comb. When lions lick each other they can remove dried blood from feeding, as well as mud, burrs, and insect pests. Lion tongues are rough enough to scrape meat off the bones of prey.

Canine teeth pierce a prey's neck or spinal cord.

Lions use their rough tongues to clean themselves.

A lion's powerful eyesight helps it hunt at night.

Like most cats, lions have excellent vision. In the bright sun, their pupils get smaller to form tiny slits. At night, the pupils expand to huge black circles, which let in as much light as possible. Inside each eye is a special layer of mirror-like cells that magnify light. Even if there is only a little moonlight, lions can still hunt.

Lions use their keen sense of smell to find water, food, and other lions. They also have exceptionally good hearing.

Social Life

Lions are the most social of all cats. They live in large groups called prides. These family groups may have only a few animals or as many as 50! Lionesses make up most of the pride. They stay with the pride into which they are born for life. Most prides are made up of one or two males who aren't related to the females, as well as about six related females and their cubs.

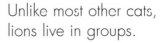

Unlike most other cats, lions live in groups.

Scientists have studied lions to learn why these animals live in groups. One benefit is that they all share the food. In a pride, different lions have different tasks. Most female lions are responsible for hunting prey and bringing meat back to their pride mates. Usually, a few females stay behind to watch and nurse cubs that are not yet ready to hunt.

Male lions protect cubs the remaining females and defend the pride's territory against intruders such as hyenas, jackals, and other lions. Male lions don't often hunt. They are slower than females due to their large size. In addition, their dark manes make it difficult for them to blend into their surroundings.

A pride's territory can range from eight to 160 square miles (12.9 to 257 km) in size. The size of a territory depends on the amount of prey in that area. If there is plenty of prey, a smaller territory can support a pride. If less food is available, lions must travel farther to hunt, and their territory is larger.

Male lions define the boundaries of their territory by spraying urine on clumps of grass,

Young lions are playful and friendly.

Lions in a pride often lie together in piles.

trees, and rocks along the border. Other lions that smell the urine scent marks know that they are trespassing and can be attacked. Male lions also roar loudly to warn strange lions away from a territory. A lion's roar can be heard more than five miles (8 km) away.

Within a pride, lions are extremely friendly. They often lie together in big, sleepy piles. Females nurse their cubs and those of other pride members. Lions wrestle and play with each other. They use their rough tongues to keep each other clean. As long as there is enough food, life in a pride is quite peaceful.

Expert Hunters

Lions hunt many kinds of prey depending on where they live. They prefer large animals such as wildebeests, zebras, antelopes, gazelles, and warthogs. Females are usually the pride's main hunters. If there are many females in a pride, they will choose larger prey so every lion in the pride has a chance to feed if the hunt is successful.

Female lions usually hunt as a team. They sneak up on their prey by crawling through the grass. Their color disguises them in the tall dry grass. Unless the wind is blowing their scent toward their prey, the lionesses can remain almost undetected.

As they get closer to the prey, the big cats form a circle around a grazing herd. One lion will make a dash for the animals. The startled herd usually runs in the opposite direction— straight toward the other lions.

Females are the main hunters in a pride.

Lions usually kill prey with a bite to the throat or neck.

These lions then ambush the sickest and weakest members of a herd. They bring down the prey with their powerful claws or teeth. The prey is killed with a bite to the neck or throat. Some lions suffocate the prey by forcing the mouth and nose closed with their jaws. The lionesses then drag the kill back to their territory.

Although the males do not take part in the hunt, they feed before the females and cubs. Often they will stuff themselves when there is a fresh kill and then not feed again for a few days. Lions can eat more than 100 pounds (45.3 kg) of meat during one feeding.

The lionesses feed together once the males have finished eating. The cubs eat last. Sometimes males take a large enough piece of meat to share with hungry cubs. As long as there is enough meat, cubs have a good life.

Sometimes, however, water is scarce and grasses dry up. During these dry periods, lions' prey may go elsewhere to find areas for grazing. When the large herds leave, lions are left with only dangerous buffalo and small prey, such as lizards, rats, and birds. If hunting is unsuccessful, lions may steal leftovers from leopards and hyenas.

When food is extremely scarce, lions in large prides hunt and feed alone.

The Mating Game

While female cubs stay with their pride for life, male cubs are forced to leave when they are about 18 months old. The young males stay together as a group for one to two years. During this time their chests become broader, their muscles grow stronger, and their manes begin to grow. Lions become fully mature at three to four years of age. They begin to look for a pride that they can take over by driving the dominant, or strongest, males away. If there is only one dominant male in the pride, then the newcomers stand a chance.

Male lions will defend their territory fiercely. The big cats often are seriously injured in fights over territory. It is not unusual for incoming males who take over a pride to kill all of the young cubs. They do this to get rid of all traces of the previous male. If a female loses her cubs, she is ready to mate again. This way, all the new cubs born into the pride will be related to the new male leaders.

A dominant male watches over the females in a pride.

Mating can take place at any time of the year, though female lions usually become pregnant only once every 18 to 24 months. Males usually mate with the lionesses in their pride. Sometimes a female will mate with a male from another pride if he can get close to her without being chased away by the top male. When a female is ready to mate she makes calling sounds and sprays urine on bushes, rocks, and trees. Her scent marks let males know she is ready. Males and females usually stay together for four to five days. They are often quite affectionate, rubbing their cheeks together and cleaning each other with rough tongues.

Because lions live together in a pride, male lions are one of the few cats that help raise the cubs. They do this largely by defending the territory and protecting the young from harm.

Male lions defend the pride's territory and protect the young.

Raising Young

Females clean a cub.

Female lions are pregnant for almost four months. Before giving birth, a lioness finds a den beneath some bushes, in a small cave, or under a rock ledge. A female gives birth to between two and five cubs. Newborn cubs weigh about three pounds and are helpless at birth. Their eyes do not open until about 10 days after they are born. Cubs look like small fuzzballs covered with spotted fur.

A lioness always protects her cubs. To keep them safe she moves them from one hiding spot to another because hyenas, jackals, leopards, and even other lions prey on defenseless cubs.

When they are two months of age, lion cubs are old enough to join the rest of the pride. At first, the small cubs appear frightened by the other lions. The roars of the big males and the playful pounces of older cubs send them running back to the protection of their mother. After some time, however, they become used to living in a pride. They spend most of their time sleeping and playing.

Lion cubs chase everything that moves: insects, small animals, and the swishing tails of adult lions. This play helps cubs develop hunting skills that they will need as adults.

Although cubs continue nursing until they are seven months old, they also eat meat after they join the pride. If there isn't enough meat to go around, cubs may go hungry. Lionesses lose half of their cubs to starvation each year.

New cubs stay close to their mother.

Cubs learn to hunt by watching adults in action.

The process of learning to hunt doesn't begin until cubs are old enough to join the pride in a real hunt. Even then, they often stay back and watch the adults. Cubs sometime practice attacking the kill when adults have finished eating.

Survival is difficult for young males when they first leave the pride. They often start by hunting small, slow animals or by stealing a kill from leopards or hyenas. Brothers stay together because they are more effective hunters when working as a group.

Humans and Lions

Male lions have always been prized by hunters.

During the last 100 years, thousands of lions have been hunted and killed by humans. Most of these hunters have killed lions and other wild animals for sport. Many animals that lions eat are also killed by humans. As a result, the prey on which lions depend is also disappearing.

There is another problem facing lions today. The huge area of land on which they live is disappearing. As the number of people in the world increases, more land is farmed and settled. That means less land for lions. In many African countries, lions are considered pests. When they stray out of their protected reserves, they are often shot, trapped, or poisoned.

Because of human activities, many lions are threatened or endangered. Humans must work to protect the natural habitats of lions so that these creatures can survive.

In India, Approximately 300 Asiatic lions are left, and live in a 560-square-mile (901-sq-km) sanctuary. It is difficult for that many lions to live in such a small area. Sometimes, lions that leave the park will prey on livestock and threaten humans. The Indian government is creating a second sanctuary to give those lions more space.

Unfortunately, unless other countries follow India's efforts to create safe sanctuaries for lions, the animals long known as the "King of Beasts" may soon lose their kingdom. It is up to humans to make sure this does not happen.

African Lion Facts

Scientific Name: Panthera leo

Shoulder Height: 4 feet, males often 50% larger than females

Body Length: 8 to 12 feet long from nose to tail

Weight: 300–500 pounds

Color: golden yellow coat, males have dark brown manes

Reaches sexual maturity at: 18 months

Gestation (pregnancy period): 102–113 days

Litter Size: 2–5 per litter

Favorite Food: zebra, buffalo, antelope, giraffe, wildebeest

Range: found in open savanna and desert areas south of the Sahara, a small population found in northwest India

Glossary

lioness A female lion.

mane The long, thick hair on the head and neck of a male lion.

prey An animal that is hunted by another animal for food.

pride A large group of lions.

reserve A protected place where animals can live and breed safely.

savanna A flat, grassy plain with few or no trees.

tuft A bunch of hair attached to the end of a lion's tail.

Further Reading

Books

Bocknek, Jonathan. *Lions* (Untamed World). TX: Raintree Steck-Vaughn, 2001.

Jordan, Bill. *Lions* (Natural World). TX: Raintree Steck-Vaughn, 2000.

Robinson, Claire. *Lions* (In the Wind). IL: Heinemann Library, 1997.

Theodorou, Rod. *Lion and Tiger* (Discover the Difference). IL: Heinemann Library, 1997.

Web Site

The Asiatic Lion Information Center—*http://www.wkweb4.cablenet.co.uk/alic/*

The Lion Research Center—*http://www.lionresearch.org/*

Index